ABSOLUTE BEGINNERS
Ukulele

To access audio visit:
www.halleonard.com/mylibrary

Enter Code
4277-3365-9368-4683

Published by
Music Sales Corporation
257 Park Avenue South
New York, NY 10010, USA

Music Sales Limited
14 - 15 Berners Street,
London W1T 3LJ, England

Music Sales Pty Limited
20 Resolution Drive,
Caringbah, NSW 2229, Australia

Order No. AM993597
ISBN 978-0-8256-3633-2
This book Copyright © 2008 Amsco Publications,
A Division of Music Sales Corporation, New York

Written by Steven Sproat
Edited by Ann Barkway
Music processed by Paul Ewers Music Design
Cover and book design by Chloë Alexander
Photography by Matthew Ward and Geoff Green
Printed in the United States of America
  by Vicks Lithograph and Printing Corporation

Images courtesy of:
Henry Diltz/Corbis (Tiny Tim), page 5
Hal Roach/MGM/The Kobal Collection (Laurel and Hardy,
  from *Sons of the Desert*), page 5
Getty Images (George Formby), page 5
Gab Archives/Redferns (Cliff "Ukulele Ike" Edwards), page 31
LFI (Joe Brown), page 31

Your Guarantee of Quality:
As publishers, we strive to produce every book to the highest
commercial standards.
  The music has been freshly engraved and the book has been
carefully designed to minimize awkward page turns and to make
playing from it a real pleasure.
  Throughout, the printing and binding have been planned
to ensure a sturdy, attractive publication which should give years
of enjoyment.
  If your copy fails to meet our high standards, please inform us
and we will gladly replace it.

www.musicsales.com

Contents

Introduction

Welcome to *Absolute Beginners Ukulele*. The ukulele has been around for more than 100 years but has been enjoying a 21st-century worldwide revival! This often misunderstood instrument will open up a whole new world to you as you explore its history, charm and versatility. The "uke" is stylish, portable and loveable... so read on!

Easy-to-follow instructions will guide you through:

- History of the ukulele

- Tuning

- Parts of the ukulele

- First chords

- Strumming

- Fingerpicking

Listen to the **CD** several times to get the hang of how the chords and exercises sound. Once you've got them in your head, playing is so much easier.

Practice is very important: little and often is best. If you can practice for just 15 minutes every day, that will make you a better uke player than practicing for two hours just once a week. Your fingers need to adjust and get used to stretching, especially for changing chords. This might be the first-ever instrument that you've wanted to learn and it will take time and patience – but it gets easier.

Get to know the names of the chords and how they are positioned. This will help build up your speed when you learn new songs, as you will start to recognize familiar chords.

The ukulele has its origins in both Portugal and Hawaii. According to various sources, back in the 1890s some Portuguese travelers made a long voyage to Hawaii, taking with them their native instruments including the *braguinha* and the *cavaquinho*. The local islanders were enchanted with the self-accompaniment that these instruments allowed and the ukulele was developed and made popular. It was nicknamed "dancing flea" or "jumping flea."

In the 1920s and 1930s the ukulele had huge popularity in the United States and Europe with most sheet music showing ukulele chord boxes. The great Laurel & Hardy even used the instrument in *Sons Of The Desert* (below).

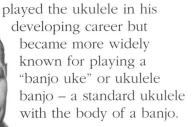

The ukulele waned in popularity during the 1950s when rock 'n' roll was emerging. However, various artists, including Tiny Tim (above), brought it back into the limelight in the 1960s, and the Ukulele Orchestra Of Great Britain (below) has helped establish the ukulele throughout the past two decades by showing how versatile an instrument it can be and how much fun can be had with it.

The late George Harrison was a big uke fan and Paul McCartney, along with Brian May, Joe Brown and Elvis Costello, have all been pictured with the instrument.

There are now other young fine exponents of the ukulele who have taken the instrument to its limits (see page 37), proving that this is an instrument worth learning.

In the UK, the comic singer George Formby (left) played the ukulele in his developing career but became more widely known for playing a "banjo uke" or ukulele banjo – a standard ukulele with the body of a banjo.

Which instrument?

There are actually four members of the ukulele family (five if you count the ukulele banjo). They are:

- Soprano
- Concert
- Tenor
- Baritone

The most popular type is the *soprano* or standard size ukulele – it's the smallest and has a higher pitch compared to the others in the family. It is usually tuned to G–C–E–A.

The next size up is the *concert,* which has a bigger body and extended fingerboard. It is tuned in the same way as a regular ukulele but is usually a little louder and more mellow.

The *tenor* size is often used when playing complicated classical or jazz pieces where "solo" chord playing and individual strings are plucked. Precision players such as Lyle Ritz, Elias Sibley, James Hill and Jake Shimabukuro tend to prefer tenor instruments.

Lastly and perhaps the least popular are *baritone* ukes. These are almost like a guitar in size but with a narrow fingerboard, and can be tuned in several ways.

The ukulele banjo (or banjo uke)
As popularized by the late George Formby in the 1930s and 1940s, the banjo uke has a much louder, harsher sound compared to the lilt of a standard ukulele.

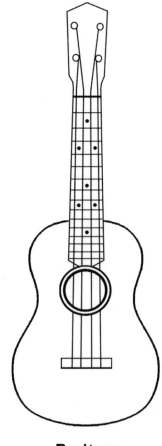

There are several tunings for this instrument. Generally the playing style is the same but certain strumming techniques work better with a banjo uke than a standard ukulele and vice versa.

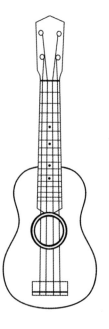

Soprano

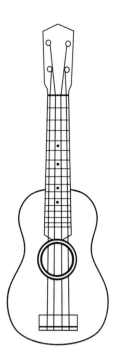

Concert

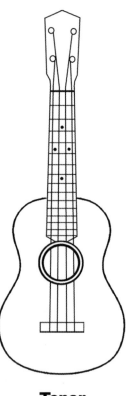

Tenor

Baritone

Buying a ukulele

These days, because of the popularity of the ukulele and cheap imports, it is possible to own a reasonably good instrument.

Try to check out a music shop that has several models to look at, and be inquisitive. Compare what you're getting (or not getting) for your money. Avoid the very cheap models, which are often brightly colored, and be prepared to move up a model or two! This ensures that your uke will have decent tuning pegs and be reasonably set up and ready to play.

Old or "vintage" instruments are extremely sought after and cost thousands of dollars, but once you've developed your playing you might wish to consider buying an old one – but do seek advice.

There are also some fine luthiers making excellent ukuleles too: Phil Davidson, Phil Cartwright and Pete Howlett are just a few makers producing high-quality ukes.

Jargon Buster

Luthier. Someone who makes or repairs stringed instruments. The word "luthier" comes from the French word for lute, *luth*.

Tip

When you're at home, keep your uke away from radiators or from open windows, but by all means, keep it out of its case and near your music stand – you're more likely to play it and practice it if it's at the ready!

Looking after your instrument

Avoid any extremes of temperature and don't be tempted to leave your ukulele in a car on a hot sunny day or overnight in the trunk on a frosty day. Invest in a decent hard case for your instrument (bags or zipped cases don't offer enough protection from weather or knocks).

Parts of the ukulele

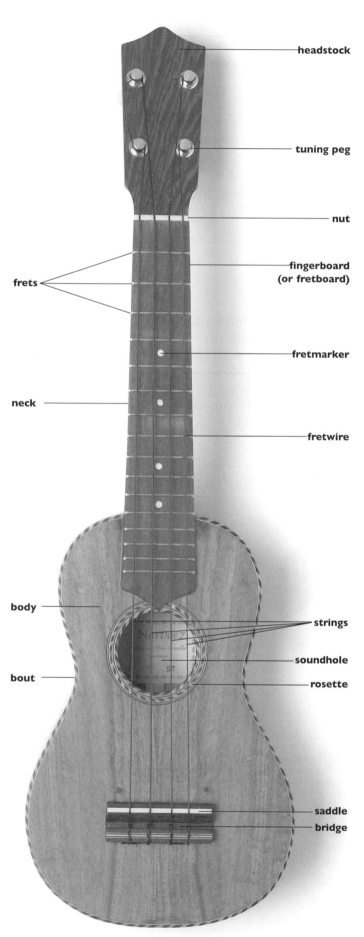

headstock

tuning peg

nut

fingerboard
(or fretboard)

frets

fretmarker

neck

fretwire

body

strings

soundhole

bout

rosette

saddle

bridge

Strings
Good quality strings can make a big difference to the sound of your instrument. It is good to experiment between brands and see which strings suit your ukulele the best.

Once you're happy, you shouldn't need to change your strings all that often (unlike a guitar). Some players keep the same ones for years!

There are clear nylon and black nylon strings, and recently a company named Aquila has produced specially developed white strings called "Nylgut." These strings (along with black nylon) usually improve the tone and give more volume on most ukuleles.

The ukulele can be tuned in several keys, but the most popular tuning is:

G   C   E   A

These are the strings in order:

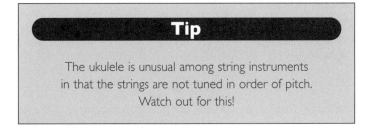

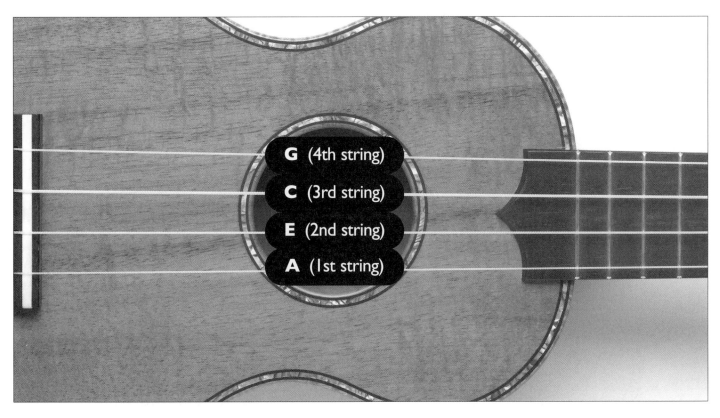

G (4th string)
C (3rd string)
E (2nd string)
A (1st string)

Tuners

There are various tuning aids available to keep your ukulele in correct tuning. Years ago, players were limited to pitch pipes or tuning forks but these days electronic guitar tuners are ideal. In particular, the "headstock" tuner (see below) is a neat, compact electronic tuner that clamps onto the end of your instrument, making it possible to tune conveniently and accurately.

You can always refer to the CD and tune to the individual strings that we play. **Track 1**

Metronome

A metronome acts as a time-keeper, and as the ukulele is mainly a rhythm instrument it is crucial to learn the secrets of keeping good time early on. There are electronic metronomes as well as traditional manual types.

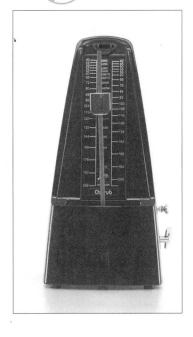

Holding your instrument

Sitting position

This is probably the easiest way to start. Sit comfortably on a stool or chair, and hold the uke just above your hip (don't allow the uke to sit on your lap).

Your right forearm should be gently "clutching" the uke and lightly pressing into the side of your body. The left hand is offering support and balance. It should be quite relaxed, with just enough pressure to keep the uke secure.

Standing position

This is harder and needs more practice (especially with a banjo uke). The same principles apply as before, but practice rising out of your chair while holding or playing your ukulele, and go from sitting to standing until you feel comfortable with how you hold your instrument. It is always better to play standing up.

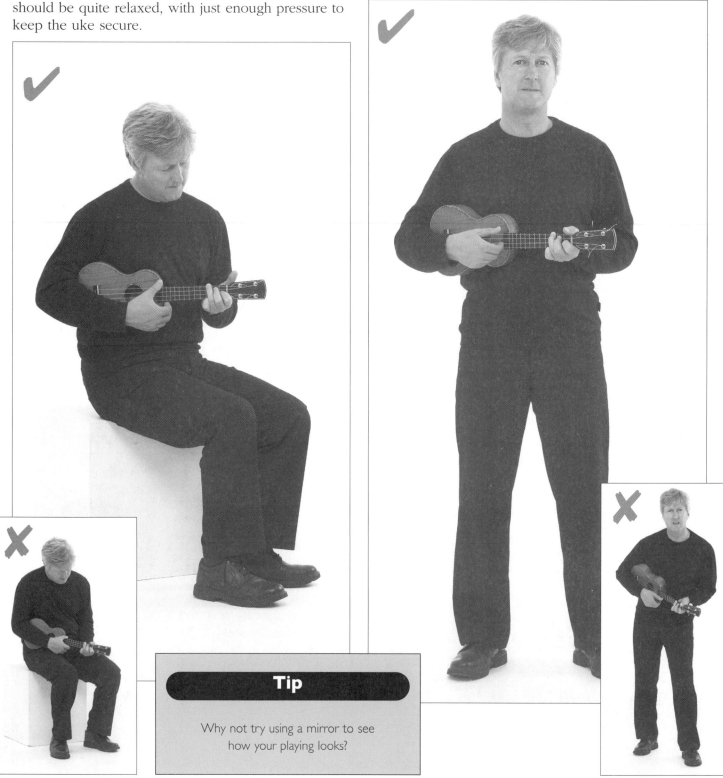

Tip

Why not try using a mirror to see how your playing looks?

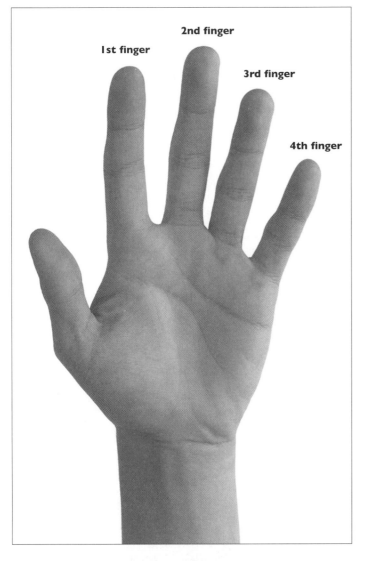

1st finger
2nd finger
3rd finger
4th finger

At first, holding down a chord will seem like a challenge. You have to be able to apply enough pressure from your fingertips and also be pressing into the fingerboard just behind the fret (not actually *on* the fret).

Your fingers will not be used to pressing down on the strings and so some chords will seem like a real effort and possibly make your fingertips a little sore. Be encouraged that your fingertips will harden with regular playing, and your fingers will get used to stretching.

Chords that once looked near impossible become less challenging!

Tip

Try to keep the nails on your left hand quite short, but allow the nails on your right hand to grow longer for strumming!

Sometimes it is okay to allow your thumb to appear to hang over the fretboard. On other chords you might find that pressing your thumb into the middle of the back of the neck works better – it depends on your fingers and the chord shape.

First five chords

Chord boxes are diagrams which represent the four strings and the first four frets from the nut.

The heavy dots indicate where to place your fingers to hold down that particular chord.

Imagine that you are looking at your ukulele fretboard as if it were held vertically in front of your face.

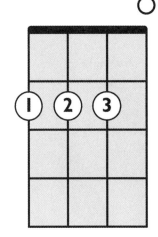

The circle above the diagram indicates that this string is to be played open.

Whenever you see a chord box, imagine turning it on its side to match the way you'd normally play your ukulele (horizontally).

Let's take a look at our first five chords: **C**, **F**, **G7**, **E7**, and **A7**.

First, the **C** chord: **Track 2**

C

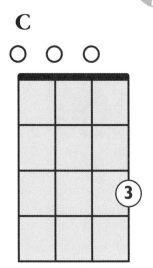

This chord box is indicating that we use our 3rd finger at the 3rd fret to press down the 1st string.

Remember to press down on the fingerboard and not actually on the fretwire.

C

Now the chord of **F**: **Track 3**

This is telling us to use our 1st finger at the 1st fret and place it on the 2nd string. Our 2nd finger goes on the 4th or "top" string at the 2nd fret. Get the hang of it?

F

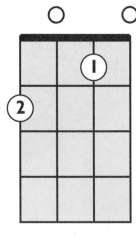

F

Try playing the chords of **A7**, **E7** and **G7** in the same way:

Track 4

A7

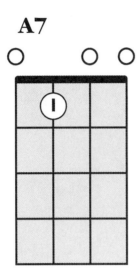

A7

Have a go at playing each of these chords, making sure that there are no "buzzes" or any "unclean" notes.

Track 5

E7

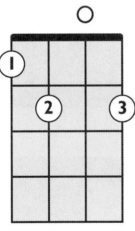

Remember to press down hard enough, otherwise you will find you are just "damping" the notes and they won't sound clean and clear.

E7

Track 6

G7

We will come back to these chords in our exercises once we've looked at strumming.

G7

Strumming

There are various strumming styles and right-hand techniques that make the ukulele quite unique. However, before learning complex strokes it is good to learn the foundation of steady basic strumming and to get used to timing.

Where to strike the strings

On a typical ukulele, the best playing area is just past the soundhole, where the last few frets on the fingerboard are. Usually the fingerboard will overlap to join the body – this is where the strings are at their lowest height from the playing area and this is called the *action*. The higher the action, the more difficult it is to play, as the risk of getting your finger caught while strumming increases – so play where the strings are lowest.

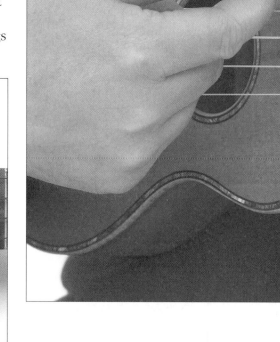

With a ukulele banjo the action can vary because of numerous body styles. Usually it is ideal to play over the skin area where the strings are lowest to the skin. If this isn't possible, it is best to play at the bottom of the fingerboard.

Hold the uke correctly, either sitting or standing, and try to develop a relaxed (almost "broken wrist") approach: nice 'n' loose. The strumming comes from the wrist, not the forearm. You might find using a mirror will help. Check that it is your wrist moving and not your arm!

If you want a good stroke to use while you're accompanying yourself singing, use the *thumb stroke.* This is a gentle, soft stroke using the ball and side of the thumb. Tuck the fingers under the neck and allow the wrist to drive the stroke – not just your thumb. It is good to use when you want to practice quietly, too!

Downstrokes

The stroke commences by striking the strings with the nail of the 1st finger (starting approximately 3–4 inches above the soundhole). You then strike the strings and follow through to be about 3–4 inches away from the soundhole in the opposite direction.

Upstrokes

The fleshy part or ball of the finger gently brushes the strings coming back up from the previous downstroke and returns to the start position – ready for the next downbeat. Put the two together and you should get a relaxed "stroking" effect, but keep it loose!

Counting beats (Downstroke)

We are going to count beats either in our head or out loud, as this will help us to keep in rhythm and help us with chord changing.

Most of the following exercises count a 1, 2, 3, 4 pattern (four beats to the bar) for every chord change. However, watch out for the part when we come to A7, as it stays on this chord for twice as long as the others in this exercise (eight beats, or two groups of 1, 2, 3, 4). You'll find most ukulele songs can be played counting 1, 2, 3, 4, but if there are lots of chords in a song you may have to shorten the number of beats on each chord to make them fit.

Because we are learning several things here (left-hand chord changes, counting beats, etc.), let's keep it fairly simple for the right hand and just play and count the downbeats. For each exercise there is a demonstration version and a backing track for you to play along with. For this exercise, there is a slow version and a fast version so that you can build up your speed and begin to gain confidence....

⊓ = **downstroke**

Walk This Way

Play this exercise through twice and then end on a C chord.

Now we are ready to try the upstrokes after every downstroke.

We still count 1, 2, 3, 4 but the beats are shortened to half-beats so that the down and up become **1** "and" – I find it helpful to count the beats as "**1** & **2** & **3** & **4** &" etc. – the "and" being the upstroke.

Tracks 11 and **12** demonstrate performances of this exercise at a slow speed and then at a faster speed. For the backing tracks, refer to tracks 8 and 10 from the previous exercise.

$\lor$ = **upstroke**

Walk This Way Tracks 11-12

Play this exercise through twice and then end on a C chord.

Let's play!

If you've never played a stringed instrument before, don't be tempted to play the melody by strumming in a style that tries to follow the tune of the song too much. Don't play the rhythm of the tune – instead, allow yourself to keep a regular rhythm with no gaps.

This way, you will recognize when to change chords, and it will sound even.

By all means play some beats with *accents* (playing them hard) or allow yourself some softer strokes if you feel it's naturally coming to you (we will cover this in a bit more detail later).

The exercise below gives you an opportunity to practice downstrokes. When you are confident, move on and play through the whole of "Rivers Of Babylon" on the facing page.

Rivers Of Babylon Tracks 13-14

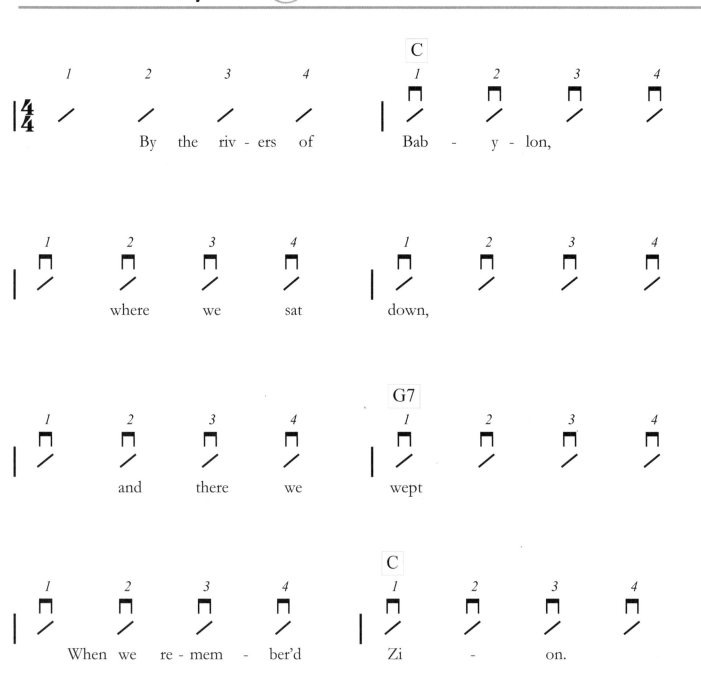

By the riv - ers of Bab - y - lon,

where we sat down,

and there we wept

When you see this symbol it means that you should repeat back to the beginning.

Fine

When we re - mem - ber'd Zi - on.

But the wick - ed car-ried us a-way cap - tiv - i - ty, re -

- quire from us a song.

How can we sing the

D.C. al Fine (with repeat)

Lord's own song in a strange land?

D.C. al Fine means go back to the beginning and play up until the word "Fine."

Nobody Knows The Trouble I've Seen

Now let's have another look at the upstroke technique that we learned earlier in the book. Listen to the example to hear how it should sound, and then give it a try.

Below is an excerpt from "Nobody Knows The Trouble I've Seen." Practice this until you are confident with your upstroke technique and then move on to play the whole piece on page 21.

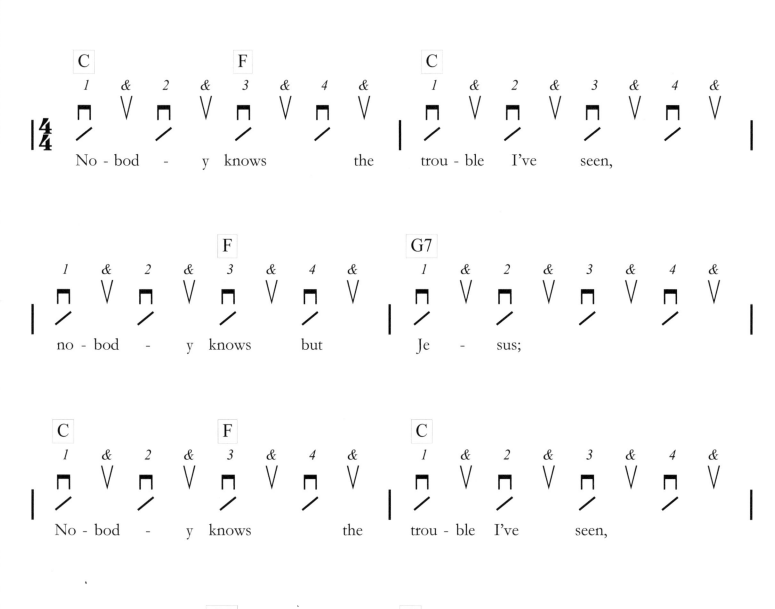

Nobody Knows The Trouble I've Seen

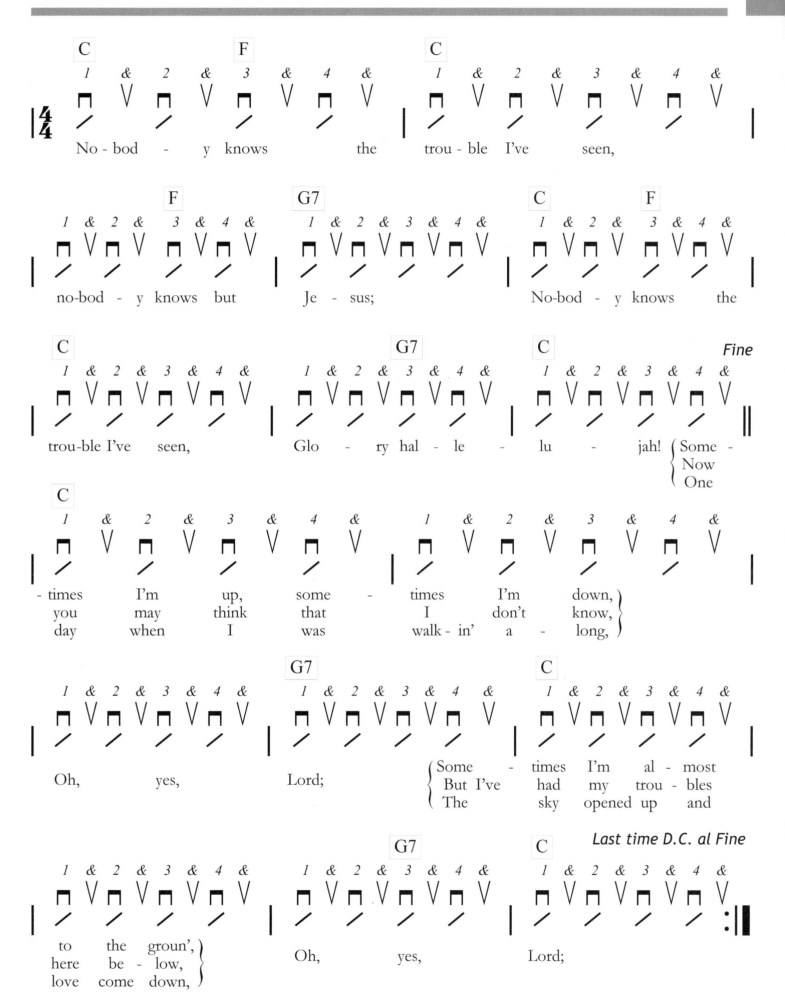

More chords

D

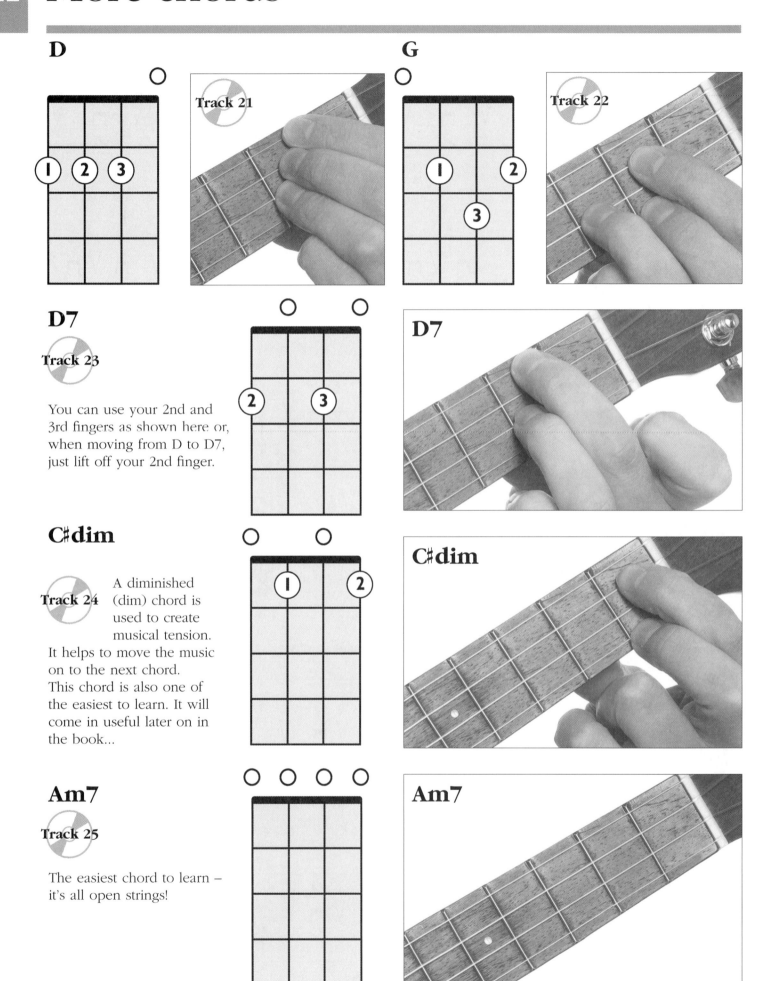

Track 21

G

Track 22

D7

Track 23

You can use your 2nd and 3rd fingers as shown here or, when moving from D to D7, just lift off your 2nd finger.

D7

C#dim

Track 24

A diminished (dim) chord is used to create musical tension. It helps to move the music on to the next chord. This chord is also one of the easiest to learn. It will come in useful later on in the book...

C#dim

Am7

Track 25

The easiest chord to learn – it's all open strings!

Am7

Later on in the book we will learn a technique called *fingerpicking*. In order to get you ready for this we will begin with a simplified version of this technique using just three strings. The style involves plucking the individual strings on each beat of the bar, creating a more fluid and perhaps more pleasant sound than that of strumming – certainly for some songs!

You will need to use your thumb (T), 1st finger (f1) and 2nd finger (f2) for this technique, and you will be plucking the 3rd string, the 2nd string and the 1st string.

The pattern looks like this:

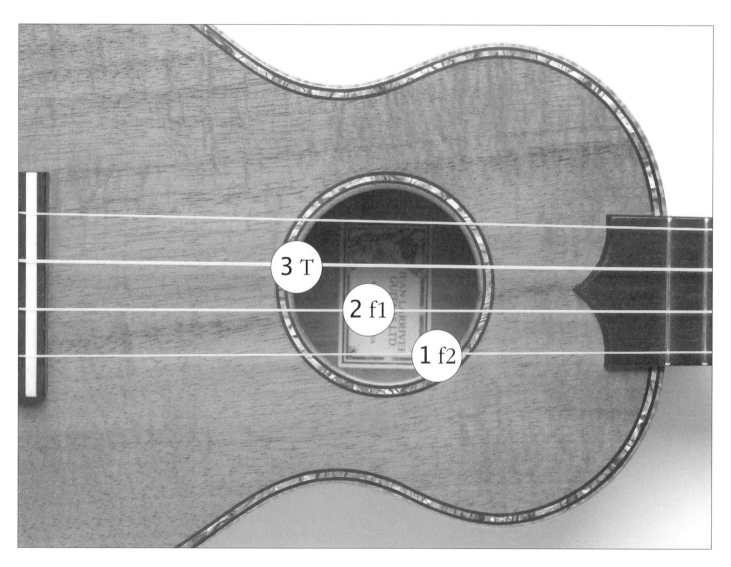

Each of the three strings should be plucked once and then you will need to repeat back to the beginning of the sequence.

The numbers in the music examples given indicate the strings which should be plucked on which beats of the bar. Hold down the chord indicated, follow the pattern above, and you should be playing a simple fingerpicking style in no time!

The first example given allows you to play the piece slowly first, as smoothly as possible, and then to speed it up when you have more confidence.

Once you have mastered the 3-string technique you can move on to fingerpicking itself.

My Bonnie Lies Over The Ocean

G				C				G							

3/4 | 3 2 1 | 3 2 1 | 3 2 1 | 3 2 1 |

My   Bon - nie   lies   o - ver   the   o - cean,   My

A7			D7					

| 3 2 1 | 3 2 1 | 3 2 1 | 3 2 1 |

Bon - nie   lies   o - ver   the   sea.   My

G			C			G					

| 3 2 1 | 3 2 1 | 3 2 1 | 3 2 1 |

Bon - nie   lies   o - ver   the   o - cean,   Oh

C			D7			G					

| 3 2 1 | 3 2 1 | 3 2 1 | 3 2 1 |

bring   back   my   Bon - nie   to   me.

3/4

G	Em	C	D7
3 2 1	3 2 1	3 2 1	3 2 1

1. In Dub-lin's fair ci - ty, where girls are so pret - ty, I
2. She was a fish - mon - ger, but sure 'twas no won-der, for

G	Em	A7	D7
3 2 1	3 2 1	3 2 1	3 2 1

first set my eyes on sweet Mol - ly Ma - lone, as she
so were her fa - ther and moth - er be - fore. And they

G	Em	C	D7
3 2 1	3 2 1	3 2 1	3 2 1

pushed her wheel - bar - row thro' streets broad and nar - row cry-ing)
each wheeled their bar - row thro' streets broad and nar - row cry-ing)

G		D7	G
3 2 1	3 2 1	3 2 1	3 2 1

"Cock - les and mus - sels, a - live, a - live, oh! A -

G	Em	C	D7
3 2 1	3 2 1	3 2 1	3 2 1

- live, a - live, oh! A - live, a - live, oh!" Cry - ing

G		D7	G
3 2 1	3 2 1	3 2 1	3 2

"Cock-les and mus - sels, a - live, a - live, oh!"

(See page 39 for Em.)

Fingerpicking

To *fingerpick* usually means to pluck individual strings in a repetitive cycle which produces an attractive, pleasing rhythm and in some cases may even help to pick out the melody of the song. There are many styles of fingerpicking involving the 1st finger (f1) and thumb (T) or using all fingers, but the finger and thumb style for ukulele is a good one and not too complicated to pull off.

The pattern looks like this, where each of the beats or half beats corresponds to one of the white circles:

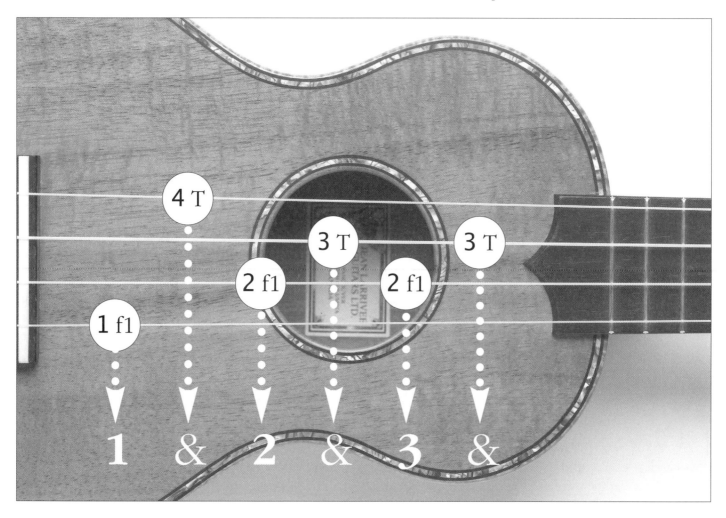

This pattern consists of six notes – one on each beat, and half beat, in every bar.

It therefore works best with songs that have three beats to a bar, as in the examples that we demonstrate on the following pages.

Try the pattern on the chord of C, as shown below:

1st string
4th string
2nd string
3rd string
2nd string
3rd string

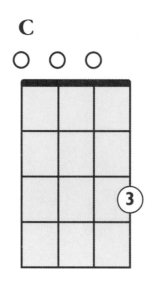

Try to take things really slowly, and aim not to pause or have any gaps after you've played the sequence.

Ideally it should be seamless, so keep playing it over and over, repeating the sequence until you almost don't even have to think about it.

Once you have perfected this technique it can be played very fast and takes on a whole new sound.

It can also be adapted to suit other tempos by shortening the sequence, and you can add interest by pinching the outer strings (1 and 4) at the same time to give accents – again, good to play around and develop some themes.

Here are the chords that you will need to play the exercise below. They are chords that you have learned already but here they show the fingerpicking pattern that you will need to use. Practice these chords individually at first before attempting the exercise shown below.

G

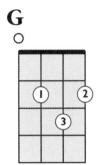 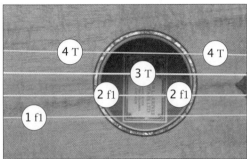

C

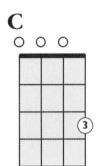 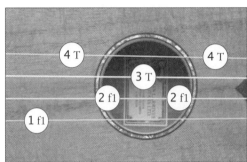

A7

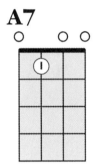 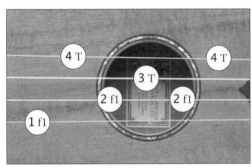

D7

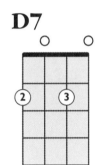 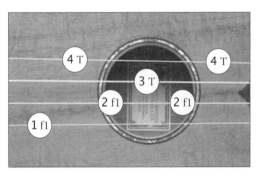

Here's an excerpt from the next piece for you to practice your fingerpicking!

End this exercise on a G chord.

My Bonnie Lies Over The Ocean

Tracks 32-33

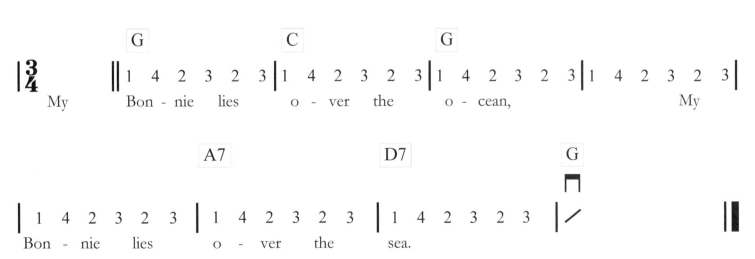

You can strum a G chord in the last bar.

My Bonnie Lies Over The Ocean

Tracks
34-37

G   **C**   **G**

$\frac{3}{4}$ || 1 4 2 3 2 3 | 1 4 2 3 2 3 | 1 4 2 3 2 3 | 1 4 2 3 2 3 |
My   Bon - nie lies   o - ver   the   o - cean,   My

A7   **D7**

| 1 4 2 3 2 3 | 1 4 2 3 2 3 | 1 4 2 3 2 3 | 1 4 2 3 2 3 |
Bon - nie lies   o - ver   the   sea.   My

G   **C**   **G**

| 1 4 2 3 2 3 | 1 4 2 3 2 3 | 1 4 2 3 2 3 | 1 4 2 3 2 3 |
Bon - nie lies   o - ver   the   o - cean,   Oh

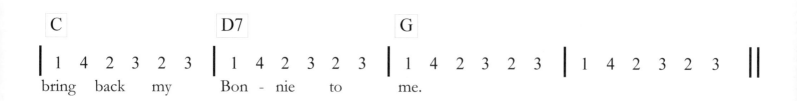

C   **D7**   **G**

| 1 4 2 3 2 3 | 1 4 2 3 2 3 | 1 4 2 3 2 3 | 1 4 2 3 2 3 ||
bring back   my   Bon - nie   to   me.

G		G7		C		A7	
1 4 2 3 2 3		1 4 2 3 2 3		1 4 2 3 2 3		1 4 2 3 2 3	
Bring		back,		bring		back,	

D7						G	
1 4 2 3 2 3	1 4 2 3 2 3	1 4 2 3 2 3	1 4 2 3 2 3
Bring back my	Bon - nie to	me,	to me,

G		G7		C		A7	
1 4 2 3 2 3		1 4 2 3 2 3		1 4 2 3 2 3		1 4 2 3 2 3	
Bring		back,		bring		back, Oh	

You can strum a G chord in the last bar.

D7			G			
1 4 2 3 2 3	1 4 2 3 2 3	1 4 2 3 2 3	
bring back my	Bon - nie to	me.	

Adding color

You are the boss of your instrument, and you can play as loudly or as softly as you want to. It is good to hear variety not only of techniques, but also loud and soft playing to emphasize perhaps a lyric or a particular rhythm.

Accents

This is the musical term given to a beat played harder than the preceding beats. Equally, backing off and playing softly exaggerates the accents when you play them especially hard – so have a go at intermingling some hard and soft strokes into your songs.

Attitude has a lot to do with how well someone might play the ukulele. It is an extension of your personality, so tell the world about yourself through your playing and develop your own style. There isn't a right or wrong way to play the instrument because the ukulele is so full of diversity and there are so many styles and techniques which all have their place.

Damping
This effective left-hand technique is worth learning. Practice putting pressure on your fingertips to execute a chord and release almost simultaneously, but do this several times in a split second. It happens very fast and gives a jazzy sound.

> ### Tip
> In music, **dynamics** usually refers to the softness or loudness of a sound or note.

Roll strokes and syncopation

There are many other techniques that ukulele players use to embellish their playing, but unfortunately there is not room to include all of these in this book. They include some of the more complex right-hand techniques such as the split stroke, the thumb roll, the fan stroke and the roll stroke.

Melody playing / solo playing

This is probably the most rewarding way of playing the uke. It encompasses lots of techniques into one piece or song. Usually the melody or tune can be heard by way of individual strings being highlighted in between clever chords and occasional strums. It usually calls for some highly complex chords which are often high up the fretboard (but not always) and where chords are changed every split second.

Chord inversions

Get to know how to play different "versions" of familiar chords so that they sound slightly different but are actually the same chord. Some chords are moveable (that means they have a shape that stays the same but slides up or down the fretboard).

It takes time to explore these but they are worth learning. People will say "What chord was that you played there?" and you can proudly say "It's the inversion of C," or whatever.

It's especially good to use inversions where you have more than one ukulele playing at the same time, so particularly in duos, trios and orchestras, etc.

The best way of learning quickly is to play songs you know in your head and know well. If you can't find a ukulele songbook with your favorite songs included, then why not get hold of a book with the guitar or piano chords in, and then all you have to do is buy a ukulele chord dictionary to see what the fingerings are for each chord.

If you can't remember the ukulele chord shape (and some of them are quite complex in pop music) then either draw your own chord box in your songbook or use a separate sheet of paper and do a chord chart for that song.

In the 1920s and 1930s, just about all popular music had ukulele chord boxes, as the uke was one of the most popular instruments in its day – it would be great if that were to come around again!

One of the many great things that the Ukulele Orchestra of Great Britain has done is to show the variety of songs that can be played on a ukulele (well, several ukuleles, actually!) The songs that the orchestra has performed include those by such artists as David Bowie, Kate Bush and Nirvana, as well as numerous classical and avant-garde pieces. So give it some thought and see what songs work on the uke – that's part of the fun of it!

On the next few pages you will find a selection of songs using the chords that we have learned in this book. You can strum these songs, or fingerpick, or make up your own style. They are for you to play around with and have fun!

Recommended listening

"Tiptoe Through The Tulips"
sung by Tiny Tim

"Leaning On A Lampost"
sung by George Formby

"Good Company"
performed by Brian May

"I'll See You In My Dreams"
played by Joe Brown (below right)

"Paul's Dance"
performed by the Penguin Café Orchestra

"That's My Weakness Now"
performed by Cliff "Ukulele Ike" Edwards (below left)

"Tonight You Belong To Me" (featured in the film *The Jerk*) performed by Lyle Ritz (ukulele) and Steve Martin (vocal)

"Miss Dy-nami-tee"
performed by the Ukulele Orchestra of Great Britain

Yellow Rose Of Texas

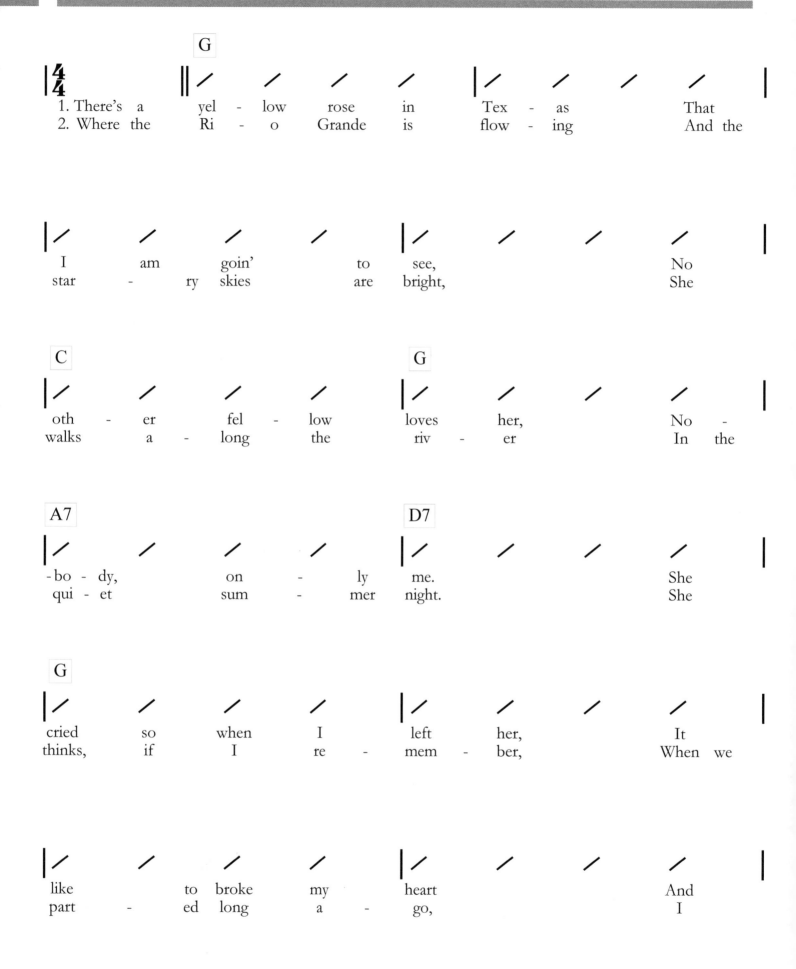

G

1. There's a yel - low rose in Tex - as That
2. Where the Ri - o Grande is flow - ing And the

I am goin' to see, No
star - ry skies are bright, She

C   **G**

oth - er fel - low loves her, No -
walks a - long the riv - er In the

A7   **D7**

-bo - dy, on - ly me. She
qui - et sum - mer night. She

G

cried so when I left her, It
thinks, if I re - mem - ber, When we

like to broke my heart And
part - ed long a - go, I

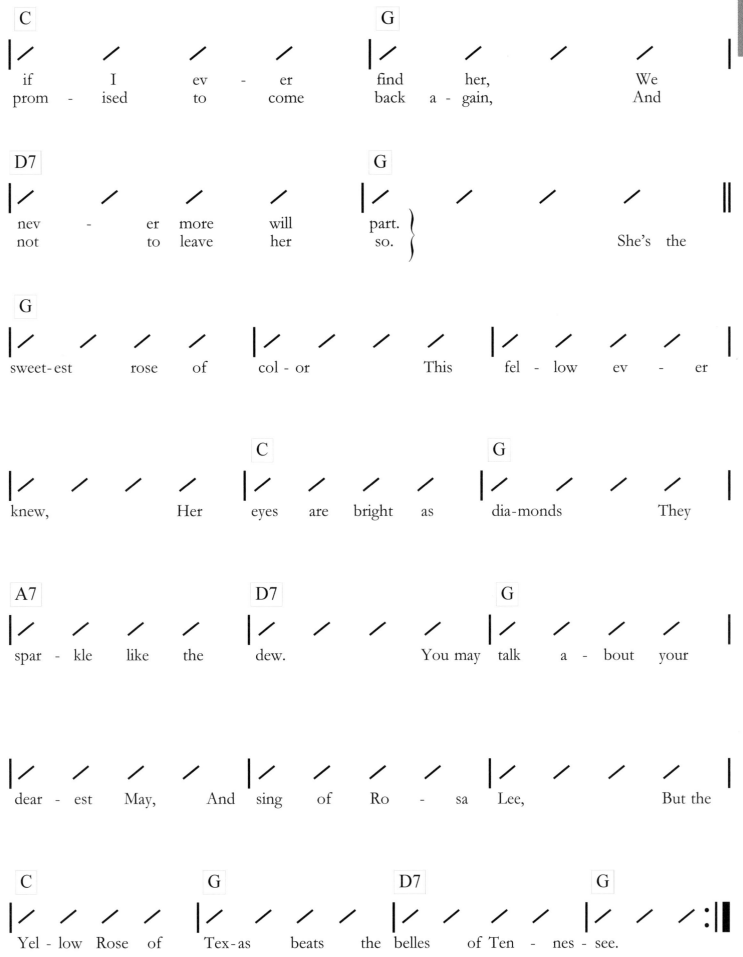

My Grandfather's Clock

2/4

D / / **A7** / / **D** / / **G** / /
My grand - fa-ther's clock was too tall for the shelf so it

D / / **A7** / / **D** / / / /
stood nine - ty years on the floor. It was

A7 / / **D** / / **G** / /
tall - er by half than the old man him - self but it

D / / **A7** / / **D** / / / /
weighed not a pen - ny - weight more. It was

/ / / / **G** / / **A7** / /
bought on the morn of the day that he was born. It was

D / / / / **G** / / **A7** / /
al - ways his treas - ure and pride. But it

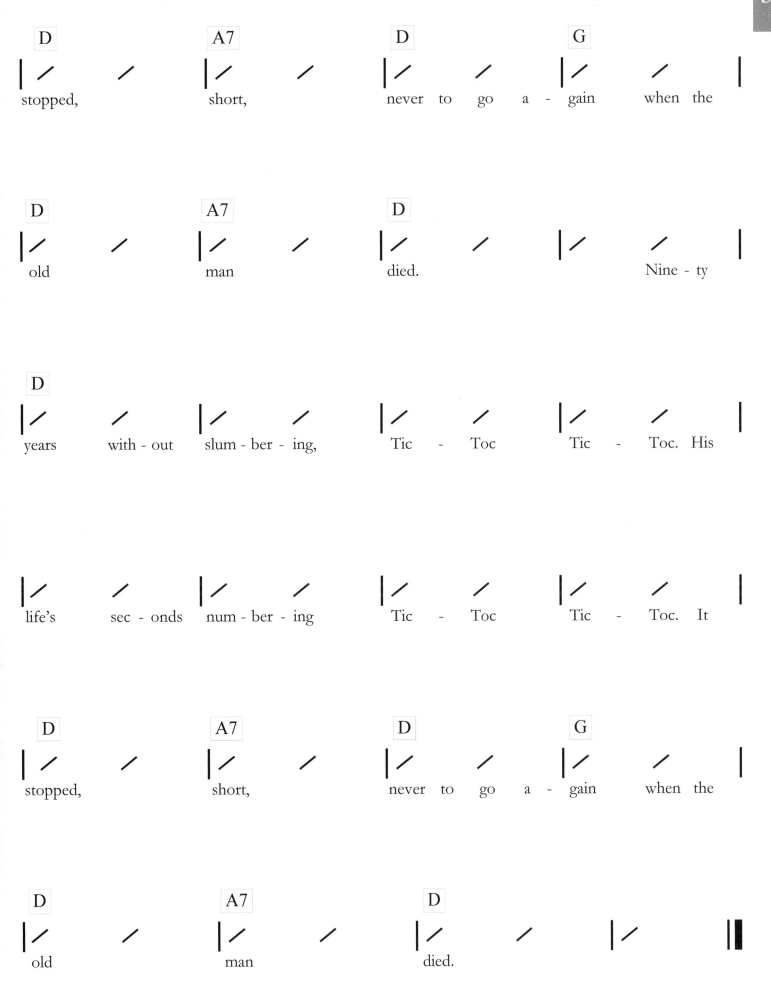

Mama Don't 'Low

This is a great tune to experiment with accents, and even adding the odd melody note in the chord.

This is a fun song (especially the way J.J. Cale did it) and should be "swung," man!

G

Ma - ma don't   'low   no   gui - tar   pick - in' 'round
Ma - ma don't   'low   no   ban - jo   play - in' 'round

here.
here.

Ma - ma don't   'low   no   gui - tar   pick - in' 'round
Ma - ma don't   'low   no   ban - jo   play - in' 'round

D7

here.
here.

G   **G7**

I   don't   care   what   Ma - ma don't   'low,   Gon - na
I   don't   care   what   Ma - ma don't   'low,   Gon - na

C   **C♯dim**

pick   my   gui - tar   a - ny - how,
play   my   ban - jo   a - ny - how,

G   **D7**

Ma - ma don't   'low   no   gui - tar   pick - in' 'round
Ma - ma don't   'low   no   ban - jo   play - in' 'round

G

here.
here.

Well, I hope you've learned more about the ukulele than you knew before you bought this book. At the end of the CD you will find a track called "What To Do." This is a song I wrote, that I hope will inspire you to carry on playing.

The fastest way to learn new styles is to keep an open mind and be like a sponge: absorb as much information as possible. Also, seek out uke clubs and societies to join.

Here are a few websites that you might find of interest:

Societies & Uke Meetings:
The Ukulele Society
www.usgb.co.uk
The George Formby Society
www.georgeformby.co.uk

Collectable Ukes for sale:
John Croft
www.theukuleleman.com
Andy Eastwood
www.andyeastwood.com

Ukulele Forum:
Ukulele Cosmos
www.ukulelecosmos.com

Uke Heroes & Ambassadors:
The Ukulele Orchestra
www.ukuleleorchestra.com
James Hill
www.ukulelejames.com
Elias Sibley
www.sibley-music.co.uk
Peter Moss
Possibly the UK's finest uke player – awesome.
Gabriella
The uke was made for her – so much talent and personality all in one person.
Ray Bernard
Long-established statesman of the uke and an instrument expert.
Andy Eastwood
Great player, talented instrumentalist (not just with his uke) and a very busy musician!
Stephen Helme
One of the finest – he taught me most of what I know.

Thank you for buying this book. I hope you meet a lot of new friends in this ukulele cosmos and enjoying playing your instrument as much as I do mine.

Happy Strumming!
Steven Sproat
www.stevensproat.com

Chord dictionary

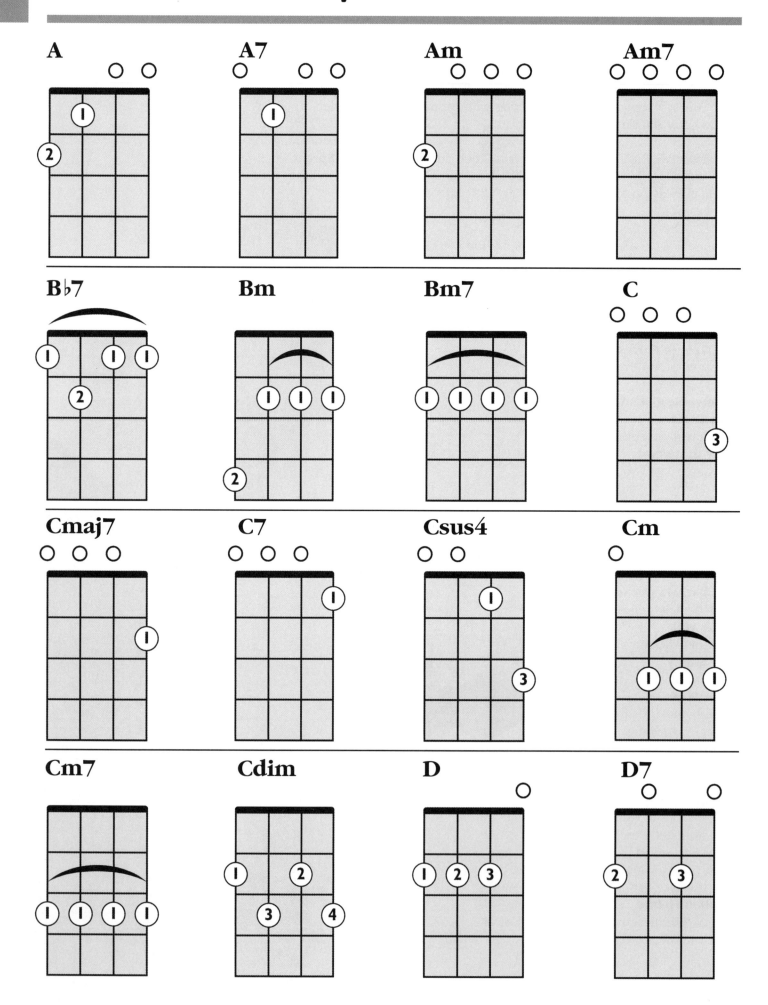

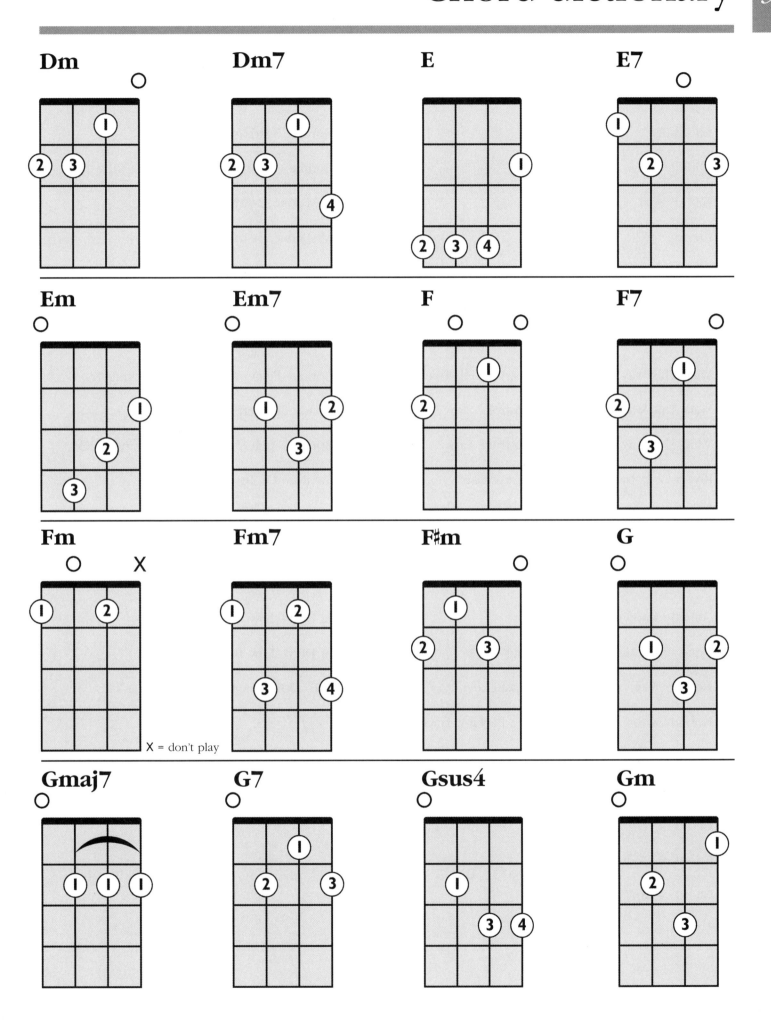

X = don't play

CD track listing